HowEx

M000195806

Freediving 101

How to Freedive and Explore the Underwater World on One Breath

HowExpert with Julie Shoults

Copyright HowExpert™
www.HowExpert.com

For more tips related to this topic, visit HowExpert.com/freediving.

Recommended Resources

- HowExpert.com – Quick 'How To' Guides on All Topics from A to Z by Everyday Experts.
- HowExpert.com/free – Free HowExpert Email Newsletter.
- HowExpert.com/books – HowExpert Books
- HowExpert.com/courses – HowExpert Courses
- HowExpert.com/membership – HowExpert Membership Site
- HowExpert.com/writers – Write About Your #1 Passion/Knowledge/Expertise & Become a HowExpert Author.
- HowExpert.com/resources – Additional HowExpert Recommended Resources
- YouTube.com/HowExpert – Subscribe to HowExpert YouTube.
- Instagram.com/HowExpert – Follow HowExpert on Instagram.
- Facebook.com/HowExpert – Follow HowExpert on Facebook.

Table Of Contents

Chapter 1: Safe Freediving Practices

Safety First & No Divers get hurt!

Freediving isn't an inherently dangerous activity, but certain safety precautions should always be in place. Keep these in mind before we go further in depth. Please, enjoy this sport peacefully and safely!

Never Freedive Alone

The most important safety procedure to follow is to never freedive alone. In case of an emergency having someone with you will save your life. Dive with a buddy. Always be conscious of where your buddy is in the water and make sure your buddy does the same for you. Make sure your buddy is wearing fins when they overseeing your dives and make sure you do the same while watching your buddy. This will rapidly increase response time in case of an emergency.

Your buddy should be qualified. Make sure they are familiar with up-to-date freediving rescue techniques, which you will learn more about in later chapters. It is always good to practice rescuing techniques, so ask your buddy if they want to join in a rescue simulation. This helps just to make sure your skills are in check.

A lifeguard watching over a pool or beach is not a qualified buddy. They may not know the proper freediving rescue techniques and they will not have an appropriate response time.

Know Your Limits

As freedivers we must push ourselves, but we must also respect our limitations. It is a fine balance. You can achieve this balance by listening to the signs of your body. Understand that if you push your limits too far you will black out or suffer from a loss of motor control. We'll go into more detail about these conditions in the later chapters, but they can be avoided by listening to your body's warning signs. Your depth and breath hold times should increase gradually. Nobody winds up at 50M overnight.

Respect Your Buddie's Limits

Make sure your buddy is familiar with freediving rescue techniques, which we will discuss later in this guide. If they are unfamiliar with freediving rescue techniques share what you know or recommend that they take a course. Stay within your limits AND your buddy's limits. They will not be able to help you if you are beyond their maximum depth.

Be Healthy

Do not smoke cigarettes before freediving. Carbon monoxide binds to your red blood cells. This means they will be able to carry less oxygen and puts you in a bad position underwater. Cigarettes will also lower your lung capacity and breath hold time.

Keep yourself in good fitness. Freediving, and preparing for a freedive, does require some exertion. Stay hydrated. Wear sunscreen. Eat potassium to avoid muscle cramps.

Never Hyperventilate

Hyperventilating may increase your breath hold time, but it comes at a great cost. We will go into more detail during the physiology section of this guide. Always take calm relaxed breaths before every dive.

Cramps

At some point in their time underwater most freedivers will encounter a cramp. It is normally in the calf. To make the pain go away grab the blade of your fin, flex your foot, and pull back gently. If the cramp is extreme your buddy may have to help you. If you are frequently suffering from cramps your fins may fit incorrectly or may be too stiff. Improper finning techniques may also lead to cramps. To prevent cramps eat bananas and other foods high in potassium.

Medical Conditions

When you sign up for a freediving course you will be given a form to fill out asking about your pre-existing medical conditions. It is important to be honest on this form and ask your instructor if you have any questions. Some conditions, such as pregnancy, lung diseases, and recurring fainting have a high risk of complications while freediving.

If you ever swallow water or experience a near-drowning event always seek medical attention. Even if you feel fine see a doctor. If there is water trapped in your lungs you may not even notice. When you go to sleep your horizontal body will move the water. It can become impossible to breathe and victims drown in their sleep. This is easily preventable by seeing a doctor.

Take a Course

This guide is not a substitute for a freediving course. Expertise from a certified professional cannot be replaced by reading a book. This is a matter of safety.

This guide is for people interested in learning more about freediving before signing up for a course. It is also for people who have previously taken a course and are looking to refresh their knowledge. This guide has some useful information that is not included in a typical freediving course. It is beneficial to all freedivers. It is NOT for people to read and then jump directly into the ocean. Remember that freediving can be potentially dangerous.

Respect the Ocean

As freedivers we must not only consider human safety. We must also consider the safety of our oceans. Make sure your behavior does not hurt the ocean. Never touch coral. The organisms that make up corals are very sensitive and touching them can kill them. Do not touch or harass marine life. Touching marine life can damage their immune system and introduce human-borne diseases to the ocean environment. Do not take any seashells from the ocean. The chemical components of shells are necessary to maintain a balanced ecosystem. Some organisms need the shells to live in. Remove any debris that you see in the ocean. Before removing it, make sure no organisms are living inside. Many fish, octopus, and other creatures take up residence inside of plastic bottles or tin cans.

Chapter 2: The Breath Hold

The Stages of Apnea

Who are freedivers?

Anyone who holds their breath underwater is a freediver. Some people just have greater levels of comfort and experience underwater.

Freediving is a great way for people to overcome water-based phobias. Those who suffered from near-drowning experiences will become empowered and liberated after learning to freedive. Tsunami victims will also benefit greatly from a freediving course. Freediving is much more psychologically demanding than SCUBA diving, and therefore much more rewarding.

Freediving is a great way to expand your knowledge of mindfulness, meditation, and mental stillness. Yoga enthusiasts are usually naturals underwater. They already have good practice with breath control, flexibility, and relaxing their mind.

Those who are passionate about the ocean should learn to freedive. Freediving is a much more natural and humbling way to interact with marine organisms than SCUBA diving. On one breath you are quieter than a SCUBA diver. This makes the fish less scared of you, so you can get closer and observe more natural aquatic behaviors. Freedivers tend to have a much deeper connection with their environment that SCUBA divers.

Freediving is a great way to meet new people! By joining a freediving club in your local area, traveling as a freediver, or joining freediving retreats you will put yourself within the social circles of other like-minded people.

Lungs

The main organ in our body's respiratory system is our lungs. This is where our bodies pick up oxygen from the air. The lungs are made up of two incredibly flexible membrane sacs in our chest. The right lung is made up of three lobes and the left lung is made up of two. They are lined with millions of alveoli, which are microscopic air sacs that exchange gases. Our lungs contain upwards of 300 million alveoli!

The average adult has a six liter lung capacity. There are some methods to increase your lung volume, which will be discussed in later chapters. Even after we exhale all the air from our lungs there is still about half a liter to one full liter remaining. This is called the residual volume.

Humans inhale by flexing a muscle called the diaphragm. You may be familiar with the diaphragm from hiccupping. Hiccups are the result of involuntary diaphragm contractions. When the diaphragm is squeezed their lungs expand to inhale. While exhaling our diaphragm relaxes.

Types of Breathing

Our lungs can be separated into three different sections. Each can be accessed with a different type of breathing: belly, chest, and upper chest.

You can see your belly rise and fall as you belly breathe. Belly breathing is also known as normal breathing. It is the most natural and relaxing form of breathing. Most humans belly breath right before they fall asleep. It uses your diaphragm to move air. For the average person their belly breaths move about half a liter of air. This may not seem like that much (considering average full lung volume is six liters), but the bottom of your lungs have a higher concentration of alveoli than any other part of your lungs. This makes belly breathing is the most efficient kind of breathing.

Children naturally breathe from their bellies. At some point adults start to breathe from their chest instead of their bellies. This may be from laziness, stress, or many other factors. During your day-to-day routine shift your attention to your breath as often as you can. Concentrate on your breath. Become aware of it. Shift from chest breathing to belly breathing. With the right amount of focus you can change how you breathe. When you change how you breathe, you change your life.

Chest breathing is the next kind of breathing. This will focus the air in your ribcage. You should be able to feel your ribcage expand and contract when you are breathing from your chest. You should have little to no movement in your diaphragm. Chest breathing uses the intercostal muscles. It can be hard to isolate chest breathing. Be patient.

Upper chest breathing is the final type of breathing. You are breathing just into the upper part of the lungs. It is very shallow. By breathing with your upper chest you are not relaxing your body. When a person suffers from a panic attack, fear, or anxiety they begin to breathe from their upper chest. Breathing from your upper chest will automatically increase your heart rate.

Before freediving practice isolating each type of breathing. This is a good way to become familiar with your lungs. Start with belly breathing. Place the palm of your hand over your belly button. Feel the rise when you inhale and the fall when you exhale. Breathe from your belly for two minutes. Then move to the chest. Feel your ribcage expand with each inhale. Feel it contract as you exhale. Breathe from your chest for two minutes. Then move to the upper chest. These should be shallow breaths. Breathe from your upper chest for two minutes, but be careful not to hyperventilate. If it helps you relax, close your eyes during this process. Notice how each breathing type changes your heart rate, mood, and energy levels.

Now that you have a better understanding of breathing we will proceed to breath holding. Any breath hold can be divided into three parts: relaxation, breath hold, and recovery.

Relaxation

Your breath hold will last significantly longer when you are relaxed. This is because a relaxed body consumes less oxygen than a tense body. That's why freedivers give themselves time to relax before holding their breath. Find your Zen. During this period of time the freediver can breathe through a snorkel, hold a buoy or pool edge, or float on their back. In order to freedive you must enter the right state of mind. Usually the minimum relaxation time is two minutes. During this time focus on releasing any tension. Tension can reside in your muscles, organs, and mind. Visualize each part of your body loosening up; start with your head, neck, shoulders, arms, torso, and make your way all the way down to your toes. Any pain or tightness will use oxygen. Clear your mind, for your thoughts waste oxygen as well.

Focus on breathing. Your inhales should come from your diaphragm. Imagine yourself breathing from your belly. The rise and fall of your stomach should be visible to your buddy. Make sure your exhales are always longer than your inhales. A good method is triangle breathing, which basically means to make your exhales twice as long as your inhales. Five to ten is a good ratio. When you feel comfortable try to inhale for five and exhale for fifteen. Count slowly. One one thousand....two one thousand...three one thousand, etc. Never rush the relaxation phase.

Once you are relaxed it's time to take your final breaths. Take one very long exhale. Do not push this too far, just consciously exhale. Try to push most of the air from your lungs (slowly!). Then take your final inhale. Start with the diaphragm and work your way up. Fill your belly, then your chest, and finally your upper chest. This should take about ten seconds. If you are spending a lot of time on your final inhale it can waste oxygen that you would use during your breath hold. Now...Hold!

Breath Hold

Holding your breath is also known as apnea. It comes from a Greek word meaning 'without breath or wind'. Ancient humans, including the Greeks, have been performing apnea for centuries. It is only within the last thirty or so years that scientists have really been studying apnea, depth and its effects on people. The field is emerging. Knowledge grows every year, so keep yourself up to date by interacting with well-informed freedivers and conducting your own research.

You should be able to open your mouth while holding your breath. Your lips do not seal the air, but your epiglottis does. That is a cartilage flap behind your tongue. It also serves to prevent your windpipe from inhaling food.

A breath hold can be divided into three stages. These stages have varying levels of comfort and discomfort. A common misconception is that this discomfort is caused by a lack of oxygen, but really it is caused by a buildup of carbon dioxide. The first a diver is comfortable, the second the diver experiences discomfort, and the third is when the diver should be heading to the surface. After the last third of a breath hold the diver will experience a loss of consciousness, which we will discuss more in later chapters. With proper technique and caution this is not something to worry about.

After the first third of the breath hold the diver will experience their first contraction. This is felt as a small, uncomfortable movement in the diaphragm. Use this sign as a guide to tell you that you have consumed 1/3 of your time underwater. Remember that this estimation is only an estimation. It will change if you are exerting yourself or thinking a lot. Over time you will become more aware of your body and understand how the different stages of apnea feel. Towards the end of a breath hold contractions will become stronger and more frequent. Just relax into them. If you freedive often you will become used to the sensation and it will not bother you.

Another feeling you may experience when holding your breath is the urge to swallow. This is natural. Just ignore it.

It is important to have a relaxed mind when you are holding your breath. If your mind is relaxed your body will follow. Imagine your thoughts are like any of your body's other processes. Digestion and other body systems shut down or slow down when holding breath (we will discuss this more in future chapters). Your body does this naturally, but it is up to you to shut down your thoughts. Feel the water on your skin, the sunlight warming your body, and whatever other sensations surround your body. Sometimes freedivers visualize other places when they start to feel uncomfortable underwater. Do not think. Feel the sensations of wherever you're visualizing. Go to your happy place. Use any meditation techniques that work well for you.

Recovery

And, back to air! Safely recovering from a breath hold takes two steps: Exhale and recovery breaths.

When you return to the surface (or when you're practicing on dry land) let out an exhale. Aim for ½ of your lung volume. This releases carbon dioxide from your body.

Next take your recovery breaths. Each recovery breath is a short, quick inhale followed by a small, passive exhale. Flex your abdomen during your inhale for a stronger recovery breath. Your lips should touch in between inhales and exhales. It should sound like you are saying 'Opah'. OOO. Paah. OOO. Paah. OOO. Pah. You can also imagine yourself saying the word 'Hope'. Your inhales should be longer and significantly stronger than your exhales. Repeat 3-5 times, even when you are practicing on dry land. Make it a habit.

Why are recovery breaths important? During apnea the chemistry of our blood changes significantly. Recovery breaths will restore your oxygen levels and bring your blood back to a neutral carbon dioxide level. By actively inhaling and passively exhaling you keep your lungs at a high volume. This promotes gas exchange.

Forming the muscle memory and habit of recovery breathing will help if you ever suffer from a blackout or loss of motor control. It may even prevent such occurrences. We will go into more details in a later chapter.

Chapter 3: Your Body at Depth

The Physiology of Freediving

Pressure Changes

Our bodies undergo changes as we descend beneath the ocean surface. In order to understand these changes we must look to physics. Scientists created one unit called the atmosphere which measures the force of pressure exerted by the air in Earth's atmosphere. For every 10 meters of saltwater depth there is 1 atmosphere of pressure. So, when you are 10 meters deep your body is experiencing 2 atmospheres of pressure. This is because you must include the pressure from the ocean, as well as the atmosphere. Apply this calculation to all depths. For example, if you are 40 meters below the surface there are 5 atmospheres of pressure on you.

Air volume decreases with pressure. Let's say at the surface you have a balloon with 10 liters in it. At 10 meters it will be 5 liters. At 10 meters the volume of air is cut in half. This is the greatest change in pressure you will experience while freediving. It is shallow, but powerful. At 20 meters the balloon will be at 1/3 of its original volume, so 3.3 liters. At 30 meters the balloon will be ¼ of its original volume, so 2.5 liters. So if you have a full lung volume of six liters at the surface and you descend to 10 meters, your lungs are already half of their normal volume (3 liters). This pattern continues as you go deeper.

At pressure gasses behave differently. The partial pressure of gases increase. Think of partial pressure as the concentration of a particular gas. SCUBA divers will be familiar with this concept. When you are 40 meters deep the partial pressure of oxygen is much higher. This will make it feel like you have more oxygen than you actually have. When a diver ascends from depth, they may think they have enough air to make it to the surface. But when they approach the changing pressures, especially around 10 meters where the pressure change is greatest, they may black out. This is called a shallow water blackout. It is much less common nowadays than it was even just a decade ago. Freediving science is an emerging field and new discoveries are keeping us safer. You will learn more about blackouts in future chapters.

The air in our atmosphere is made up of 21% Oxygen, 78% Nitrogen, and 1% trace elements. The partial pressure of Oxygen at 10 meters is 42%. Partial pressure increases with every additional atmosphere of pressure.

Pressure changes can seem like a daunting, abstract concept. Here is a table to give you a better understanding and notice the patterns of the pressure changes at depth:

Depth	Pressure	Air Volume	Air Density	Partial Pressure of Oxygen
Surface Level	1 Atmosphere	1	1	21%
10	2	1/2	X 2	42%

Meters	Atmospheres			
20 Meters	3 Atmospheres	1/3	X 3	63%
30 Meters	4 Atmospheres	1/4	X 4	84%
40 Meters	5 Atmospheres	1/5	X 5	1.05%

Airspaces

Most of our body is made of liquids and solids which resist pressure changes. However, humans have air spaces in our middle ears, sinuses, and lungs. We also create an air space when wearing a mask. As pressure increases these air spaces shrink. In the next chapter you will learn about how to deal with this change by equalizing.

Squeeze

Barotraumas, or squeezes, are pressure related injuries. They can occur if you do not use proper technique or fail to equalize. The pressure imbalance can lead to mild or severe pain. Freedivers may experience squeezes in their sinuses, ears, throat, and lungs. Squeezes in the sinus or ears are felt when you cannot equalize. These squeezes are normally resolved when the pressure gradient decreases again.

Throat squeezes arise when we do not tuck in our chins at depth. If you have 5 atmospheres of pressure on your body and look to see where the bottom of the line is, you are putting yourself at great risk for a throat squeeze. Your trachea will be exposed to the pressure. Always dive with your chin tucked in and your eyes facing directly forward. If you must look in a different direction move your entire body.

Improper form (not tucking in your chin and hunching your shoulders at depth) may result in a lung squeeze. Pushing yourself too much can also result in a lung squeeze. This is the most severe of all the squeezes. You must give your body time to adapt to greater pressures. Below 25 meters, do not add more than 3 meters of depth to your personal depth in each session. Make many dives over several days to your new personal best before proceeding deeper.

If you experience a lung squeeze you will not know until you reach the surface. Our lungs do not have any nerve cells in them, so even though the event is serious you will not feel any pain. Once you reach the surface you will begin coughing up blood. This blood will be bright red, because it is highly oxygenated.

Avoid exertion after suffering from a lung squeeze. This means do not pull up the line before heading back to shore. Have your buddy do it. You may also need your buddy to tow you back to shore. You will notice even small activities leave you out of breath. You may become unconscious after even just a small amount of exertion, so it is a good idea to stay out of water. This will last for a long time, at least one month.

If you experience a lung squeeze you must seek medical attention. See a qualified physician as soon as possible. You cannot freedive for at least one month. Before freediving you will have to see a doctor again and get medical clearance. Lung squeezes are serious complications. Freediving before your body has healed can be fatal. Repeated lung squeezes will result in chronic conditions. Lung squeezes are not a rite of passage to becoming a well-rounded freediver. Many professional freedivers with world record titles have never experienced a lung squeeze in their whole careers.

Self-awareness is the best prevention against lung squeezes. Your limits will change from day-to-day depending on your stress, rest, and relaxation. Respect your limits. Our limits are psychological and physiological. There is no reason to go deeper if your mind is not ready. You may panic, twist, and end up squeezing your lung. If your body is not ready to adapt to greater pressures you will almost certainly squeeze a lung. Gradually increasing depth and doing the appropriate stretches can prepare your body to go deeper. We will discuss stretches in a later section. If you are not relaxed do not dive. If you are stressed or shivering do not dive. If you are anxious on the surface your anxiety will be tenfold at depth. Do not freedive for numbers. Freedive for peace.

Oxygen and Carbon Dioxide

Nearly all of our body's actions require oxygen (O_2) and create carbon dioxide (CO_2) as a by-product. When we hold our breath O_2 levels drop and CO_2 levels increase. By relaxing underwater you reduce your O_2 uptake and CO_2 production. Remember that even your thoughts use O_2 and create CO_2, so clear your mind before every dive.

A relaxed body with a slow heart rates circulates blood slower. When you are relaxed your muscles, tissues, and organs require less oxygen. Think of it this way, if you are laying down your breathing is slow. When you are not exerting energy your body is using less oxygen, so it doesn't need to breathe as often or as heavily. If you are sprinting your body will naturally breathe faster. When you are exerting a lot of energy, your body needs more oxygen to support the movement. This means when you are relaxed you naturally use less O_2 and create less CO_2.

During a breath hold you will experience discomfort and an urge to breathe. This is from rising CO_2 levels, which makes your blood more acidic. You will experience diaphragm contractions and sometimes the urge to swallow. Carbon dioxide is a useful tool underwater. Use these reactions to gauge when you should return to the surface. Our CO_2 levels increase during strenuous exercise. It is important to rest between every breath hold so your body has time to return to neutral CO_2 levels. Rest for at least twice as long as your dive time.

Only when our oxygen levels are very low do we experience the signs of hypoxia. Hypoxia occurs when you are dangerously low on oxygen. Signs include tunnel vision, ringing in the ears, and a feeling of warmth. You must push your limits very far (or hyperventilate) to experience hypoxia. It is very dangerous and if you experience these signs, surface immediately and signal your buddy. Before diving again analyze why you experienced these symptoms.

Hyperventilation

Hyperventilation is defined as breathing at a rate that results in more air than you need to maintain neutral CO_2 in your blood. Hyperventilation varies depending on activity. A rate of breathing that is considered hyperventilating during rest is not considered hyperventilating during a sprint.

It is a myth that hyperventilation stores more O_2 in your blood. Our blood is naturally saturated with 95-99% oxygen. You will not be able to store more. In fact, hyperventilation inhibits your body from using O_2 properly. When your CO_2 level is lower than normal your red blood cells bond more strongly to O_2. So your blood will be circulating, but your tissues that need it will not be able to receive the O_2. Hyperventilation also raises your heart rate, which is bad for relaxation.

When scientists discovered this the rate of blackouts among freedivers significantly decreased. It used to be common for freedivers to hyperventilate before a dive.

When your carbon dioxide levels are lower you can significantly delay the urge to breathe. Diving may seem easier. This is dangerous, because we need the urge to breathe to remind us when to come up. Carbon dioxide may be uncomfortable at times, but it keeps you safe underwater.

Monitor yourself for the symptoms of hyperventilation during your breath hold. Symptoms include euphoria, metallic taste in mouth, lightheadedness, tingling extremities, dizziness, and numbness around mouth. If you experience any of these symptoms end the dive. Monitor your breathing. Make sure you are breathing at a relaxed rate. Do not perform strenuous activities right before apnea. Do not dive again until the symptoms subside and you give yourself adequate time to relax.

Nervous System

Our nervous system coordinates our actions. It activates responses in our bodies. Our bodies make many actions without us even having to think at all. For example our heart rate, digestion, and oftentimes our breath occur involuntarily. These actions are controlled by the autonomic nervous system.

There are two main divisions in the autonomic nervous system. First is the parasympathetic nervous system. The parasympathetic nervous system activates 'rest and digest' reactions. It decreases our heart rate and relaxes our muscles. Our body is able to enter a calm state. We will be able to digest food in our intestines when the parasympathetic nervous system is activated. The sympathetic nervous system is the other division of the autonomic nervous system. It is responsible for 'fight or flight' responses. This causes our muscles to contract and our heart beat to quicken. Our thoughts will begin to race. This comes from a deep survival instinct to react appropriately to danger.

Our bodies are never relying on completely one or the other autonomic nervous system functioning, but we can definitely shift to one majority. So, which nervous system do think it is better to engage while freediving? The parasympathetic nervous system is better, because it helps us relax. How do we do select which autonomic nervous system is active? We can change between the parasympathetic nervous system with our breathing patterns and our thought patterns. Belly breathing activates the parasympathetic nervous system. This is why if you alter your breathing you will truly alter your whole life. Reassuring thoughts also activate the parasympathetic nervous system. Remind yourself that you are safe, still, and at peace. Your body listens to your mind. If you think there is danger around your body will automatically shift into the sympathetic nervous system. Chest and upper chest breathing will also activate this nervous system. If you did the exercise to isolate different parts of your lungs you probably noticed a feeling of adrenaline or unease after two minutes of upper chest breathing. This is your instinctual reaction. Freedivers must have an intimate understanding of their bodies to be graceful in the water. Change your breathing and your thoughts to relax and become one with water.

Chapter 4: Everything about Equalization

Equalizing your Air Spaces

When to Equalize?

Equalizing changes our air spaces to match ambient pressure. As previously discussed, freediving forces our bodies to undergo massive pressure changes. To adapt to these changes we must equalize air spaces as they shrink on descent. There's no reason to worry about equalizing on ascent. During ascent excess air will be released involuntarily.

Make sure you equalize before feeling pain. For most people this means equalizing every meter. You will need to equalize more often when you are shallow than when you are deep. Usually if you are able to equalize at 10 meters you will be able to equalize all the way to your target depth. Since the volume change of gases decreases the deeper you go you will need to equalize more often in the first 10 meters than you will from 40 to 50 meters. Do not continue your descent if you are unable to equalize. This can result in a sinus squeeze or a burst ear drum. It is okay to descend slowly and pause to equalize. Never force an equalization.

If you are freediving with a hood you must take extra precautions. If air becomes trapped between your ear and the hood it will become impossible to equalize underwater. You can flood your hood with water before the dive. You can also invest in a hood that is designed with holes in place to facilitate water flow. Do not cut holes into your freediving hood by yourself. The neoprene will begin to rip and the holes will grow into tears.

The more you practice equalization the easier and more comfortable you will be underwater.

Ears

If you have ever flown in an airplane you have had to equalize your ears before. At high elevation, in mountains or in tall buildings, you must equalize as well. Under pressure the membrane in our middle ear bends inwards. This can create discomfort and in extreme cases cause pain. Equalizing uses air to push the membrane back out to its normal position. In an airplane you may have equalized by swallowing or wiggling your jaw. There are some different techniques to use underwater, since the pressure is much greater.

Freedivers are at a high risk for ear infections. Always rinse your ears out with clean freshwater after diving. If you're suffering from an ear infection do not go diving. Treat it with antibiotic ear drops and wait until the symptoms go away.

Frenzel

Frenzel is one method to equalize the middle ear and sinuses of freedivers. This is the best way to equalize when diving on one breath. To perform Frenzel:

1. Pinch your nose
2. Close your mouth
3. Press the tip of your tongue against the back of your teeth
4. Move the back of your tongue gently upwards (imitate the action used to create 'T' sounds)

You should feel your middle ear expand. Frenzel is performed with no diaphragm movement. Practice on dry land. Frenzel can be performed to around 35 meters.

To make sure you are doing Frenzel and not another method of equalizing, place one hand on your diaphragm. If it is still you are doing Frenzel correctly. The Adam's apple is another good way to tell if you are doing Frenzel. It should go up and down as you complete the exercise. This is much easier to notice in men than in women.

On deeper dives you will want to strenghten your Frenzel. You can do this by stretching your tongue. A strong tongue can perform a strong Frenzel. Practice Frenzel often, even on land. There are some tools you can use to make your tongue stronger, such as a funnel that goes into your nose that you can blow into a balloon with. Once the balloon is full control the air with your tongue as it escapes through your mouth. Since the movement is so subtle it may be hard for you to be sure that you are doing Frenzel correctly. As your instructor for advice.

Valsalva

SCUBA divers will be familiar with the Valsalva equalization technique. Valsalva equalizes the middle ear and sinuses. It is much easier to master than Frenzel, but not ideal for freediving. To perform Valsalva:

1. Pinch your nose
2. Close mouth
3. Exhale gently

You should be able to feel the change in your ears. Practice on dry land.

It is recommended that freedivers opt for Frenzel instead of Valsalva. This is because Valsalva takes air from the lungs and Frenzel uses air that is already in the mouth. It also requires more energy (and more oxygen) than Frenzel. Valsalva can be performed to around 20 meters, but once again, it is not a good idea.

If you place your hand on your diaphragm and do a Valsalva equalization you should be able to feel movement.

Hands Free

Some freedivers and SCUBA divers are able to equalize their middle ear and sinuses without pinching their nose. This requires motor control of the Eustachian tubes, which connect to the middle ear. It is estimated that only 10% of people are able to learn this skill, but there are many facial expressions and stretches to help. Ask your instructor to give you advice. You can also look up informative videos on the internet. If you are eager to learn no hands equalization practice during a feet-first descent. Hands free equalization can be performed to about 35 meters.

Mouth Fill

For dives deeper than 35 or 40 meters Frenzel will no longer be able to equalize the middle ear and sinuses. There is just not enough air in the mouth to perform this task. Deep divers must use a mouth fill technique. They move the air from the lungs into the mouth. This is a highly specialized technique that you must take a course to learn.

Mask

Remember that if you are diving with a mask that also creates an air space. If your mask is not equalized it will create a sucking sensation over your eyeballs. To equalize the mask exhale a small amount of air from the nose. Do not exhale so much that a lot air bubbles leave the mask, as all air is precious during a breath hold. Equalization is one reason it is important to invest in a low-volume mask. Many divers do this naturally without having to think about it. SCUBA divers are familiar with this practice.

Stretching for Equalizing

To make equalizing easier and more comfortable stretch before your dive. Stretch your jaw by making large, over exaggerated chewing motions. Stretch your ears by equalizing on land a few times. If you are tense equalizing will be difficult. Always remember to relax.

Reverse Block

Do not dive if you are experiencing congestion. Usually you won't be able to descend very far if you are suffering from congestion. Equalization will become impossible when mucus is blocking air flow to your sinuses and ears.

Even if you are able to equalize on descent, the mucus may prevent excess air from escaping on ascent. When this excess air has no escape it causes something called a reverse block. Divers who experience a reverse block spend days in pain and are unable to board an airplane.

Avoid decongestants. If you use a decongestant then go diving you are putting yourself at a very high level of risk for a reverse block. At pressure medicines wear off quickly, so even if your descent is fine you may encounter mucus and congestion on the ascent. If you are taking decongestants with the hope to go diving within the next few days it is still a bad idea. Often decongestants have a rebound effect and as soon as you stop taking them the congestion comes back.

To make congestion go away there are some things you can do. First, avoid air conditioning. Air conditioning makes the air around us very dry. Our sinuses will compensate by producing extra mucus. Eat herbs and food with anti-inflammatory properties, like turmeric, black pepper, pineapples, and thyme. Drink a lot of water, as this can help flush out the mucus. Always stay hydrated. Water will also boost your health and keep you from becoming congested again in the future. Some breathing techniques for congestion will be discussed later.

Chapter 5: Rescue

How to Save a Life

How to be a Safe Buddy

Communication is key between freediving buddies. Make sure your buddy tells you how deep they plan to go, how long they plan on taking, and what technique they will use. These three points should be discussed before every dive. You should understand exactly what is required for you as a buddy. Usually for the warm-up dives buddying is passive. This means you can stay on the surface, hold onto the buoy, and observe the dive. For deeper dives buddying is active. This means you must meet your buddy at a certain depth, discussed before the dive. When you meet your buddy underwater stay across from them, so you can monitor their ascent. Most freediving accidents occur in the top 1/3 of the ascent, so this is a good depth to meet your buddy. If 1/3 of the target depth is less than ten meters, meet the diver at ten meters anyway. Remember what we discussed about shallow water blackouts? You will be able to respond quicker to a blackout if you meet the diver at ten meters where the pressure change is very strong.

What should you look for as a safety diver? Three keys: monitor the eyes for panic, examine the diaphragm for contractions, and check if the diver's lips are turning blue from hypoxia.

If a diver is in trouble you will notice several things. Panicked eyes, blue lips, and strong contractions are some giveaways. Look for a change in finning style. They will go from smooth, strong kicks to weak ones. In other situations may also speed up towards the end of the dive. This diver is not relaxed. They may even be suffering from panic. Exhalation is another sign of an emergency, as a freediver should never exhale underwater.

Remind your buddy to do recovery breaths after the dive. Do not ask questions or let them speak until they have completed recovery breathing.

Sometimes you will be asked to be a buddy for a diver performing static apnea. This is when they are face down in a pool holding their breath. Just like any other buddy situation, communication is key. Some divers want their buddy to talk to them and motivate them. Others wish for their buddy to be silent, so they can enter a state of extreme calm and stillness. Observe your buddy closely and point out any areas of tension you notice after their dive. Perhaps their shoulders were tense after their first contractions.

The main task while static buddying is to perform a safety check. This will differ depending on the buddy team, expected breath hold time, and other factors. Usually you will tap your buddy on the shoulder at a set interval and they are expected to give you a sign that shows they are okay. For example you may tap them on the shoulder every minute that passes. If there is no sign tap them again. If there is still no sign bring them to the surface. Instead of tapping you may also speak or come up with form of signaling. Remember to make sure your buddy does recovery breaths.

You should take buddying as seriously as you take your own diving. Your buddy is counting on you. Be present and alert. Communicate effectively. When both buddies are actively engaged in their roles they form an effective buddy team.

Emergency Action Plan

Before engaging in any potentially dangerous activity you should form an emergency action plan (EAP). It is common for participants in extreme sports to make an EAP. Hikers, mountain bikers, kite surfers, and even SCUBA divers partake in this precaution. An EAP will give you a solid foundation to appropriately respond in an emergency scenario. Some people freeze up when they are in an emergency, but simply writing down information or making a checklist can free their mind to react appropriately. This will put your mind at ease and make sure you're prepared for any problems that may arise. An emergency action plan will vary depending on the situation. The standard emergency plan will include an ambulance contact number, location of the nearest hospital, and protocols. Make sure you have an emergency contact phone number for you buddy.

An emergency action plan when diving off of a boat will include marine radio protocols, how to get in touch with the local coast guard, and the location of certain safety equipment, such as an AED, fire extinguisher, and EPIRB. If you are freediving on a charter boat or other service, they will have an emergency action plan. Ask to see it.

For freedivers who are going very deep (50 meters or deeper), it is good idea to have emergency oxygen close by in case of decompression sickness. You must still seek a hyperbaric chamber if suffering from decompression sickness, but it is a good idea to breathe emergency oxygen on the way there. We will discuss decompression sickness and freediving in the upcoming pages.

It is a good idea to have a first aid kit stocked before entering the ocean. In addition to the average first aid kit it should include vinegar and razors in case of jellyfish stings, tweezers in case of sea urchins, and antibiotic cream in case of reef cuts. Reef cuts are very likely to become infected and should be washed extremely thoroughly.

Remember that freediving is a generally safe activity and these are just smart precautions to take. Do not be scared, because then you will lose your relaxed state of mind.

Treating Barotraumas

Barotraumas are pressure related injuries. They include squeezes. Failure to equalize is the most common cause of barotraumas. You should seek medical attention if you're experiencing extreme pain in the ears, sinuses, teeth, or other facial areas after diving.

One of most severe barotraumas is a burst ear drum. You will have to spend one month or more out of the water to give your ear time to heal. It will be very painful. Burst ear drums are prone to infection, so your doctor is likely to give you antibiotic ear drops. An infection will keep you out of the water longer.

Reverse block is another serious barotrauma. Always seek medical attention when suffering from a reverse block. We discussed reverse blocks above, but will go into more detail now. The air you used to equalize on descent becomes trapped by mucus on ascent. It is incredibly painful. There is not a lot you can do to reduce pain when suffering from a reverse block. It may last for several days. Drink lots of water, eat foods high in anti-inflammatory properties (pineapple, thyme, turmeric, and black pepper). You must wait for the mucus to move and release the pressure. Those suffering from reverse blocks cannot board airplanes, as this can make the pain excruciating and result in permanent damage to the ears or sinuses.

The best way to prevent barotrauma is using common sense when diving. Dive with proper form, do not force equalization, and do not dive with congestion.

Decompression Sickness and Freediving

All SCUBA divers are familiar with decompression sickness (DCS). This occurs when pressure changes rapidly and gases (mostly nitrogen) in our body do not have time to dissolve. The gas bubbles will grow as the pressure decreases. Imagine the chemical reaction that occurs when you shake up a can of soda and open the lid. A similar reaction occurs in the body. This is why SCUBA divers ascend from their dives slowly. Treatment for DCS involves sending the afflicted diver to a recompression chamber, a long and expensive process. Decompression sickness can be fatal. Often one of the first questions avid SCUBA divers ask when taking a freediving course is "Will I get decompression sickness from freediving?"

While it is possible to contract decompression sickness while freediving, it is extremely unlikely. It is not something to really worry about until you start diving below 50 meters. When divers are going that deep they usually limit themselves to one or two deep dives a day to prevent DCS.

Avoid freediving right after SCUBA diving. Wait for at least 12 hours. If you are doing multiple dives or decompression dives wait for 24 hours. The rapid pressure changes your body encounters while freediving can lead to decompression sickness, because your body may still be dissolving some gasses. On SCUBA your body accumulates tiny bubbles in your tissues. You must give these bubbles adequate time to dissolve. It is completely safe to freedive before SCUBA diving. This is true, unless you are doing deep dives. In that case, exercise appropriate precaution.

If you are experiencing decompression sickness never try to recompress your body by freediving or SCUBA diving. You must seek the expertise of a doctor qualified to operate a hyperbaric chamber. It is a good idea to become familiar with the location of your local hyperbaric chamber. This information should be in your emergency action plan.

What is a Loss of Motor Control?

A loss of motor control (LMC) occurs when the diver has reached the surface. It is caused by hypoxia. A diver suffering from an LMC is in the danger zone of low oxygen before losing consciousness. Sometimes divers underwater will experience a loss of motor control before blacking out.

How do you recognize an LMC? It is sometimes referred to as a "samba", because the diver will make jerky movements. Usually the head, hands, and eyes are most affected. A weak LMC will be just the head and the eyes. A strong LMC will affect their whole body and make it impossible for them to keep their airways out the water by themselves.

A diver will only experience a loss of motor control when they push themselves or hyperventilate. Stay within your limits and take your time relaxing and breathing deeply before every single dive.

Respond to a Loss of Motor Control

If you are responding to an LMC the top priority is to make sure the diver keeps their air spaces above the water. Failure to do so may result in drowning. You also want to protect them from injury. Oftentimes a diver having an LMC in a pool will injure their head on the pool edge. Prevent this by following appropriate safety protocols.

First, remove the diver's mask. This will make it easier for them to breathe. If the afflicted diver does not breathe appropriately their LMC will turn into a blackout.

If in a pool, move the diver away from the pool edge. Support the diver's shoulders and head. Make sure their airways are out of the water. One way to do this is to wrap your arm beneath their armpit and support their head with your palm. If you are on the right side of the diver, use your left arm, and vice versa. This gives you a lot of control over the diver.

If you are freediving on a buoy use the buoy as a support system. Position the diver so they are facing away from you, between your body and the buoy. Wrap your arms beneath their armpits and grab the buoy firmly. This is a strong position and you can easily support the diver.

Gently remind the diver to do recovery breaths and say their name. When they come back to their senses do not let them speak, not until they do recovery breaths. The risk of blacking out is high, so they must restore oxygen in their blood. Just tell them do recovery breaths and breathe.

A diver who suffers from an LMC will not always realize it is happened. They may not even know that anything is wrong and want to continue diving. Monitor your buddy closely, stay calm, get out of the water, and explain to your buddy what you observed.

Always be responsive. If you think someone is having an LMC do not hesitate. React and respond, their safety depends on it. It is much better to respond when it is unnecessary than fail to respond when someone really needs it. Some people fail to respond to emergencies, because they are low on confidence. Remember adequate care delivered is always better than perfect care withheld.

A diver who suffers from an LMC should not dive again that day. They should analyze their depth, times, preparation, and relaxation in order to figure out why they had an LMC before diving again.

A serious LMC may lead to a blackout. Learn how to prevent and respond to a blackout in the next section.

What is a Blackout?

When the body runs out of oxygen, it will black out. This is a loss of consciousness where your body shuts down all functions not necessary for immediate survival. Blackouts can happen in pools, in the ocean, and anywhere. They can even occur on land, but this is rare. The urge to breathe will be very strong before blacking out, so most people will involuntarily start breathing on land before they black out. If you black out on land you will eventually come back your senses on your own. If you blackout in water you will drown if nobody rescues you. Always hold your breath in water under supervision. An expert or a beginner can black out.

Blackouts only happen when you push yourself or hyperventilate. Some world champion freedivers who reach depths of 100 meters have never had a blackout. Listen to your body. Never hyperventilate. Be cautious.

There are some warning signs before you are about to experience a blackout. If you notice any of these symptoms underwater, surface immediately or make an indication to your buddy. Usually when you start to experience these warning signs it is already too late and you're going to black out. Remember the biggest warning sign to a blackout is pushing your limits. You will be experiencing an extreme urge to breathe and very strong contractions before you reach a blackout.

The signs are different for different people, so be cautious if you notice anything abnormal. Many divers report ringing in their ears. It will start as a small hum and escalate in loudness. You will also feel warm. Typically it starts in your head or neck and makes it way down your body. The dive will start to feel easier and you will be deceived into thinking you are okay. You will experience tunnel vision or a total loss of sight. Thoughts will be fuzzy and incoherent. This feeling is comparable to narcosis for SCUBA divers.

To notice a blackout in your buddy the biggest sign to look for is an exhalation. Freedivers never exhale underwater, but it is involuntary to release some CO_2 after blacking out. You will also notice the diver stop moving.

Respond to a Blackout

When a diver blacks out their larynx (a muscle in the throat) will close up to prevent the inhalation of water. This is called a laryngospasm. It usually lasts for one minute, although everybody is different. After one minute the laryngospasm will stop and the diver will begin to inhale water. Sometimes safety divers refer to this as the 'Golden Minute'. Usually for hypoxic blackouts the injured person has three minutes before they start losing brain cells. Blackout rescues are time sensitive. If you think you need to respond do not hesitate.

Blackouts can occur when a diver reaches the surface or underwater. A diver may experience a blackout on the surface if they push themselves and fail to perform adequate recovery breaths. Always remind your buddy to perform recovery breaths, especially after reaching new depths or times. If a blackout occurs underwater, your top priority is to get the diver to the surface.

Position yourself so the diver is perpendicular to you. Use one hand to support the back of the diver's head. Use the other hand to support the chin. This action will keep their mouth closed and prevent the inhalation of water. It is best to use your palm, so your fingers can keep their mask in place. Their mask is helping them by keeping them from inhaling water through their nose. Once you have one hand on the back of the diver's head and one hand on the chin you can begin swimming up. It is best to extend your elbows to make for an easier ascent. This will also give you more room to kick. Do not make jerky movements, as this can result in neck injury.

This is why buddy communication is important. If a diver blacks out a depth you're not able to reach it may be impossible for you to rescue them. Respect your buddy's and your own limits. Never dive deeper than your buddy's maximum depth.

Once the diver is on the surface the first thing you should do is recovery breaths. It may have been strenuous for you to bring the diver back up to the surface and we don't want one blackout to turn into two.

While doing your recovery breaths remove their mask. Our bodies will recover from a blackout when the subconscious realizes it can breathe air again. Our face has many sensitive nerve receptors. Removing the mask will expose the diver's face to wind and sunlight, thus helping their subconscious realize that they can breathe. Also you want to make sure the person is able to breathe from their nose when they recover.

After removing the mask focus on supporting the diver. Your top priority is to keep their airways out of the water. A good way to do this is to wrap your arm beneath their armpit and support the back of their head with your palm. If you are in a choppy ocean position yourself so the waves crash onto your back and you can protect the diver's face from being splashed.

BTT is an abbreviation used for the next step in rescuing a blacked out diver. It stands for blow, tap, talk. These three steps stimulate the sensitive nerve cells on the face to remind the diver that they are on the surface. Blow on the divers face. Aim for the area just beneath their eyes. Next, tap the diver in this area. Your taps should not be too gentle. Finally talk. Repeat the divers name and remind them to breathe.

After ten to fifteen seconds of BTT, if the diver has not regained consciousness, start recovery breaths. In order for a recovery breath to be successful their head must be in the right position. If one arm is already supporting their shoulders and head, use the other arm to pinch the nose and push the forehead back. By pushing the forehead back you are opening their airways. It is important to keep the diver's head out of the water, so they don't swallow water. While pinching the nose blow strongly into the diver's mouth. Repeat every five seconds.

If the diver is still unresponsive you need to get them onto dry land. You cannot perform CPR on a diver in the water. In a pool this is easy, but in the ocean you will have to tow them to shore or the nearest boat. Choose whichever is closer and easier to access. Remove their lanyard before beginning the tow. Remove their weights if they are not positively buoyant at the surface, as they should be. If the diver was overweighted it will explain why they blacked out, because it takes a lot of energy to ascend with too much weight. Tow the diver by supporting their head and chest and kicking beneath them. While towing the diver remember to do rescue breaths, say their name, remind them to breathe, and keep their airways out of the water.

If five rescue breaths do not resuscitate the diver you must being cardiopulmonary resuscitation, also known as CPR. CPR involves a series of chest compressions and rescue breaths. It would be helpful f there are two responders, so one can do BTT and one can perform CPR. Remember the first step of CPR is to alert emergency medical services. Take a CPR course to become confident in this life-saving skill.

Usually a diver will recover from a blackout within about three seconds of reaching the surface. If they do not recover at that time they are likely to recover after the first rescue breath. The first rescue breath may be all it takes for the laryngospasm to cease and the diver to regain consciousness. It is extremely rare for a diver to need more than one or two rescue breaths. It is even rarer for a diver to need to be towed or to need CPR.

A diver who suffers from a blackout is done diving for the day. Repetitive dives may lead to repetitive blackouts. The diver may be confused and not really understand what happened. Help them get back to shore or out of the pool and calmly explain to them what you witnessed. There is no such thing as a mystery blackout. If you black out analyze your depths, whether you were hyperventilating, stress, fatigue, dehydration, and other factors. Blackouts occur when you push yourself too much. Alter your diving to make sure it doesn't happen again.

Remember these steps:

1. Bring diver to the surface
2. Remove their mask
3. Keep their airways are out of the water
4. BTT (blow, tap, talk)
5. Rescue Breaths

Chapter 6: The Blue Mind and Body

Your Mammalian Dive Reflex and how it helps you Underwater

What is the Mammalian Drive Reflex?

Every freediver knows their breath hold time is longer underwater than it is on dry land. Why? Our bodies have a physiological response to water that allows us to hold our breaths longer. It is called the mammalian dive reflex (MDR). This is a response shared by all mammals. The same response that allows marine mammals, such as whales and seals, to hold their breath for extended period of time, is activated in humans, but to a lesser degree. This response is present and involuntary in all humans. Even if you have never attempted apnea, swam in the ocean, or gone freediving, the mammalian dive reflex is active in you. It helps submerged organisms conserve oxygen and use it more efficiently. As you train more in freediving this response will become more pronounced. Over time the response will be stronger and it will be activated quicker.

Freediving medicine is a growing field. There are still a lot of questions to be answered about the MDR and its effect on physiology, breath holds, depth records, etc.

Lower Heart Rate

When submerged in water our heart rate lowers. This helps preserve oxygen by circulating blood at a slower rate. You can observe this on your own by relaxing and holding your breath on land and monitoring your heart rate. Then submerge your face in water (under buddy supervision) and record your heart rate. Your heart rate will be lower in the pool. This exercise can only be performed when you are relaxed. When you are not relaxed your heart rate is high even when you hold your breath.

Carbon dioxide makes our blood more acidic. Your blood continuously circulates throughout your body. Once highly acidic blood reaches the cortex this response in particular will be triggered. This is your body helping you dive. This response will also slow your metabolism.

Peripheral Vasoconstriction

Vaso means blood vessel. So peripheral vasoconstriction is when the vessels of extremities (periphery) shrink. During freediving this occurs to reduce blood flow. Blood flow will be focused on the essential organs: brain, heart, and lungs.

Legs and arms will still be able to function without oxygen for some time. They will begin to produce lactic acid. The more you use extremities at depth the more anaerobic (without oxygen) fuel they will use. Continuous deep dives may make you considerably weaker and sorer than activities on land that exert the same amount of energy. Practice will help your body tolerate higher levels of carbon dioxide.

Blood Shift

At a certain depth our lungs shrink to a point where they would collapse. This depth varies on an individual's lung volume. Just a few decades ago scientists were sure that at this depth no freediver could survive. It was thought that the lining of the lungs would touch and tear and cause certain death. Some brave freedivers kept pushing this depth limit. The scientific community was shocked when they emerged on the surface completely fine and healthy.

Upon reaching a certain depth the capillaries, or small blood vessels, surrounding the alveoli are engorged with blood. The volume of blood in the capillaries protects our lungs from becoming injured.

The blood shift is so strong in some whales that they actually exhale before descending. The blood shift is able to protect their enormous lungs to extreme depths.

Splenic Shift

Our spleen is a small organ which stores red blood cells, white blood cells, and other things. During apnea the spleen will release red blood cells into the bloodstream. These are highly oxygenated and help you hold your breath longer.

Some tribes in Indonesia and the Philippines have been freediving for generations. They freedive to gather food from the ocean. It is an essential part of their survival and culture. Scientists have found that members of these tribes have spleens up to twice as large as the average human. This is a remarkable feat of evolution. It enables these people to hold their breath longer. Some members of these tribes have also adapted to see perfectly underwater without a mask.

Immersion Diuresis

At depth your body will perceive excess blood volume. We already discussed peripheral vasoconstriction. This phenomena will lead to an increase blood volume in the chest. Your body will think there is too much fluid and its natural reaction will be to generate urine. Your kidneys will get to work and suddenly you will have the urge to pee.

It is completely natural and unavoidable to pee in your freediving wetsuit. If you are renting a wetsuit, someone else has already peed in it! Sometimes it is better to buy your own gear. Clean your wetsuit with anti-dandruff shampoo to prevent the growth of fungus. This fungus may cause a skin rash.

We lose a lot of water while freediving. Sweating in a wetsuit, breathing through the mouth, and immersion diuresis leave us less hydrated. Be sure to drink plenty of water before and after your dives. You can even store a water bottle in your buoy to drink between dives. It is impossible to live healthily when your body is not properly hydrated.

Initiate

Different factors can trigger the mammalian dive reflex. We already discussed that rising CO_2 levels will cause your heartbeat to slow down. This usually makes your first breath hold the most challenging. This is because your mammalian dive reflex is still kicking in and your heartbeat is faster than it will be on the following breath holds. Immersing your face in water has the same effect and causes bradycardia.

Rising pressure causes peripheral vasoconstriction, as well as the blood shift.

Low temperatures can trigger the mammalian dive reflex. This is one of the benefits of diving in cold water. However, once you start to shiver your body will be using more oxygen. Whenever you start shivering it is time to get out of the water, because your dives will become increasingly difficult and increased exposure to cold water may lead to hypothermia.

Water itself can trigger the MDR. Take off your mask before a dive to allow the water to touch your sensory nerves. The sound of bubbles and waves can also trigger the appropriate responses. It may help to nhale on the surface and exhale underwater so you can hear your bubbles and feel them float across your ace.

Chapter 7: Relaxation

Techniques to Stay Calm under the Waves

Why do Freedivers need to Relax?

Sometimes freediving is referred to as 'extreme meditation'. The benefits of relaxing underwater are immense. In fact, freediving would be basically impossible without some good relaxation techniques. Remember to take your time relaxing before freediving. Also give yourself plenty of time to relax between dives.

Keep it Slow

Slow, fluid movement will help you blend in seamlessly to the water. Avoid jerky actions. Do not try to descend and ascend as fast as you possibly can. This will stress you out and waste oxygen. It will also be more difficult to equalize and enjoy your dive. Freediving is not a race. Find a rate that is feels good, then go slower. By going slowly you conserve oxygen and give your body time to equalize. Speed will only burn through oxygen and occupy your mind with stressful thinking.

Stay in the Moment

When you are descending do not think about the depth. Do not think about how deep you are, how deep you want to go, or deep you have been. Focus only on the present moment. Pass no judgements onto yourself. Enjoy the sensations of freediving, and you will find yourself naturally at the bottom of the line with very little effort.

If you are having trouble keeping your mind from worrying with thoughts like 'How many meters until the bottom?' 'Am I close to the surface' and 'How deep am I right now?' there are some techniques you can try. First, try closing your eyes. Feel the water flow across your body. Relax. Clear your mind. If you are not comfortable closing your eyes underwater try focusing your eyes on something specific. Choose something directly in front of you. Look at the line. Watch the strands weaving together as you go up and down. If you are diving on a reef wall examine the fish and corals. Or if you are in the open ocean, just focus on the big blue surrounding you. Blue is a color that naturally calms the mind, so try to let your thoughts disappear.

Guillaume Nery, champion freediver from France, said something very wise in regards to this. He said "Never look at the surface, with your eyes or your mind."

Visualization

Visualization is a powerful technique used by top performers in a wide variety of fields. Everyone from

Olympians to top military personnel use visualization to increase their physical skills. Visualization is especially handy for freediving, because we are entering a world that is completely foreign to us. No matter how often you dive the underwater world is still a strange place. Many people find it uncomfortable to be underwater. Visualization can be the key to relaxing our subconscious minds. It is a meditative process.

For visualization to be successful you must convince yourself that you are really doing the activity. Lay down, take deep breaths into your belly, and create a scenario in your mind. Engage your five senses. Imagine the taste of the saltwater and your rubbery snorkel. Imagine the smell of the saltwater. Scent is the most powerful sense for visualization. Some Olympic athletes apply sunscreen before visualizing succeeding in their sport. Then before participating in the sport they will apply the same sunscreen. This will bring them back to the relaxed and confident state of mind they entered during visualization. Next, think of the things you will see while freediving. Sight is another powerful sense. Imagine the color of your fins. See the waves as they splash through the water. Imagine the fish and the corals. Visualize the deep blue colors of the ocean. See your buddies swimming alongside you. Next visualize the sounds you associate with freediving. Do you hear the crackling sounds of a coral reef on your way to the dive site? How about the gentle sound of waves lapping against the shore? Imagine the sound of your breath. You may even imagine the funny sound of someone laughing through their snorkel. Imagine the sound of silence when you are deep underwater. This calms may people. Then move to feeling. Imagine the feeling of and on your feet as you walk to the ocean. Feel the sensation of the sun warming your skin. Feel your wetsuit sticking to your skin. Visualize the sensation of the water as you enter. Imagine how it calms you...

Once your mind has entered the setting begin to visualize your dive. See yourself relaxing before the dive. Remind yourself of the wonderful sensation of focusing on nothing but breathing. Then imagine your descent. Think of it as smooth and effortless. Your equalization technique works perfectly. It is easy. See the colors of the rope as you descend. See the deep blue all around you. Feel the water flowing across your face. Hear the silence that will embrace you underwater. The dive is relaxing. Your form is hydrodynamic and you glide through the water. You are not thinking about depth or numbers, only the sensations you will experience on the dive. You begin to free fall. The water gently pushes you down. Everything is smooth. Suddenly you reach the bottom of the line. You are comfortable and make your turn. The ascent feels great and close to the surface you begin to float up. Your ears feel good. Your body feels good. You are back on the surface. Imagine your recovery breaths. Imagine your buddy smiling, the color of the buoy, the landmarks on the shore. Only think of positive, fulfilling experiences during visualization. Visualization may occur in the first person or from a different perspective. Just visualize however feels natural to you.

Do not hold your breath while visualizing freediving. This may cause negative associations between your mind and the sport when your experience the urge to breath. During this practice simply continue to breathe into your belly.

It can help to smile while visualizing. This will ease any anxieties you may have. A smile sends signals to your mind that is okay to relax. Once your mind knows it is okay to relax the rest of your body will follow. If you are visualizing with this relaxed feeling, you will find yourself especially calm when completing the activity. It is also a good idea to smile during your relaxation period before a dive.

Practice visualizing with other activities and visualizing for freediving will become easier and more natural.

Hangs

Some divers like to do hangs at depth. It can be very relaxing. This is when you hold onto the line and relax underwater. It is a good way to observe marine life and connect to the ocean.

Use caution when doing hangs below 15 meters. This is not recommended, because the partial pressure of the oxygen is higher at such depths. You will feel like you have more air than you really have at depth.

Chapter 8: Equipment

The Gear that allows us to Dive

Freedivers should choose gear for comfort and function. You should flow through the water effortlessly. Make sure the fit is correct by going to your local freediving school and trying on the gear. Ask a professional for some advice.

It is better to purchase your own gear than to rent it. Rental equipment is not always well taken care of. It may also fit improperly. It is a hassle to switch masks and fins between dives. It can also slow your progress as a freediver to constantly wear a different mask that doesn't fit perfectly. You will be much more comfortable underwater when diving with your own personal set of gear. It will also give you more opportunities to dive whenever and wherever you want.

To save some money you can buy second-hand freediving gear. Ask your local freediving school if they have any second-hand equipment for sale. Another good place to check is the internet. Go on craigslist to find some good deals (if you live in an area where freediving is popular there will be more results).

Freshwater rinses after every dive will keep your gear in good condition. Store freediving gear in a cool, dry place. Make sure it is never exposed to excessive sunlight. UV rays can degrade the materials of fins, masks, buoys, and most gear. Wetsuits are especially sensitive to sunlight. Always hang wetsuits in the shade. Do not store equipment in a parked car or hot garage, as ongoing heat will also degrade the materials.

It is a good idea to read the manufacturer's handbook before diving with any new equipment.

Masks

To conserve oxygen look for a mask with a low volume. A smaller air space means you will need to use less air to equalize your mask. Low volume masks are also more hydrodynamic than high volume masks. A mask that is perfect for SCUBA diving may be cumbersome for freediving.

A mask that fits correctly will form a seal around your face. There is a way to test this before going into the water. Put it onto your face without the strap, suck in air through your nose, and let go. An improperly fitting mask will leak and be uncomfortable. It is better to buy a mask in person rather than on the internet, so you can check for the fit.

If you take good care of your mask it should last for years, even decades. Before going underwater with your mask there are some things to consider. First, all new masks come with a filter on the inside of the lens. Remove this filter before diving in order to prevent fogging. No amount of anti-fog can prevent a mask from fogging if it still has the filter. Toothpaste is the best way to remove the filter. Cover the inside of each lens with toothpaste. Leave it there for five minutes.

Then rinse the mask thoroughly. Repeat this process 3-7 times. Another way to remove the filter is with heat. Some divers use a lighter to melt off the filter. We recommend toothpaste, because it eliminated the risk of damaging the mask.

Before diving make sure your mask has the proper fit. Adjust the strap so that it is not tight. Loose is the way to go. A mask that is tight on the surface will be way too tight under pressure. It may seem paradoxical, but a mask that is too tight will actually be leaky.

It is okay to freedive with contact lenses. Just be careful not to take off your mask and open your eyes or open your eyes when your mask is flooded. It may be more comfortable to invest in a mask with your prescription in it.

It is popular for SCUBA divers (especially those who frequently dive from the shore) to wear masks with tinted or mirrored lenses. This prevents UV rays from harming their eyes or impairing their vision. Never freedive with these masks. It may prevent your buddy from recognizing signs of an oncoming emergency.

Whenever you take off your mask always defog it. Even if it was just hanging around your neck for two minutes you must defog it. Defog your mask by spitting into each lens, rubbing it around, and rinsing it in the ocean. Saliva is the best defog. Avoid paying for commercial defog as it really never works as well as saliva. Baby soap can be a good alternative, but if you do not rinse the mask thoroughly it can sting your eyes. Never wear your mask on your forehead between dives, as this will lead to an especially foggy mask.

Also, a mask on your forehead is the international sign for a diver in distress.

Snorkel

The snorkel is attached to your mask and allows you to breathe at the surface. It is good for relaxing and taking deep breaths on the surface. Your snorkel should never be in your mouth underwater. We will go into more detail about the reason for this in an upcoming chapter.

For freediving choose a simple snorkel. Do not buy a snorkel with a purge valve on the bottom, as these frequently break and cause leaks. Avoid extra bulky snorkels, as they will be less hydrodynamic. Most freedivers prefer a hard snorkel to a soft snorkel. Some snorkels have a 'splash guard' on the top. This can be useful in choppy conditions, but is not necessary for all freedivers.

Wetsuits

Freedivers use wetsuits for buoyancy, thermal protection, and protection from the environment. They are made from a material called neoprene.

When choosing a wetsuit make sure you find something that is comfortable and allows your body to be flexible underwater. Freediving is a sport that requires a wide range of motion, so you will be frustrated if your suit limits your actions. Your wetsuit should not cut off circulation to your hands, feet, or neck. For the perfect fit, invest in a custom wetsuit. There are many high-quality wetsuit dealers where you can send your measurements and they will craft a suit that fits your exact body shape.

Wetsuits keep us warm by allowing water to enter the suit, trapping it, and using our body heat to heat up the water. A well-fitting wetsuit should be snug, so it can properly trap the water. A loose wetsuit will allow water to flow around freely and cannot properly warm you. Wetsuit thickness is measured by millimeters (mm). When choosing wetsuit thickness consider not only the temperature of the water you are going to dive in, but also how long you will stay in the water while freediving. Usually it is better to wear a thicker wetsuit while training, because you spend time still, relaxing on the buoy, and monitoring your buddy. While recreational freediving you will be a little warmer in the same temperature water, because you will spend more time swimming. You should also consider your own personal tolerance to the cold.

Freediving wetsuits vary a little from SCUBA wetsuits. The traditional SCUBA wetsuit has a zipper in the back. Since zippers aren't very hydrodynamic freediving suits are designed differently. They are in two pieces. First are pants that reach about a divers belly button. Then is the top is pulled over the shoulders. It is like a long-sleeved leotard and a button at the bottom fastens it in place. Often, a hood is connected to the top. As long as it fits correctly, a SCUBA diving suit is perfectly fine to wear freediving. You just won't see competitive freedivers donning SCUBA wetsuits. It is impossible to freedive in a SCUBA dry suit, because of the air space.

Remember that as the wetsuit thickness varies, so will the amount of weights that you require. Wetsuits are incredibly buoyant. Even in warm water some freedivers prefer to wear a wetsuit and weights, because it gives them more control over their buoyancy.

Wetsuits come in two lengths: full and short. Full wetsuits cover the body from wrist, to neck, to ankles. Short suits stop at the elbow and knees. Typically freedivers wear full-length wetsuits, because they are more hydrodynamic.

Fully body wetsuits do a great job protecting us from underwater hazards. When freediving in an area with abundant jellyfish be sure to wear a wetsuit. It can be hard to relax and find your inner zen while being stung. Wetsuits are also useful when exploring sunken shipwrecks. Be careful, because most wetsuits will not protect against sea urchins, sting rays, and other organisms. These animals should not bother you unless harassed anyway.

There are three different neoprene variations that freediving wetsuits are made out of: closed cell, open cell, and smoothskin.

Closed cell wetsuits are strong and durable. The neoprene is protected by a strong outside lining. This can be made of nylon or lycra. They are used by surfers, SCUBA divers, and freedivers. They are versatile. You will be able to use a closed cell wetsuit for many other watersports than freediving. Also, you will save money. Closed cell wetsuits are the least expensive of all freediving suits. They are available in one piece or in two pieces. That being said, they do have some drawbacks. The outer lining may prevent complete flexibility underwater. They may not keep you as warm as long as other wetsuits, because water flushes in more often. These wetsuits are good for beginners.

Open cell wetsuits are hydrodynamic and beautiful. There is no outside layer on the neoprene, so it touches your skin and the water directly. Open cell wetsuits have a lot of benefits. You will have better range of motion and flexibility in an open cell wetsuit. They are incredibly elastic. They also have stronger insulation than closed cell wetsuits. This is because the neoprene touches your skin directly. Less water will flush through the suit. The open cell design is more hydrodynamic than the closed cell. They are great for underwater photography, because they have a little luminescence to them that comes out really well in photos. Most competitive freedivers compete in open cell wetsuits. Usually open cell wetsuits come in two pieces, so this is preferable for freediving. However, open cell wetsuits do have some drawbacks. They are considerably more expensive than traditional wetsuits. They are also more fragile. Be careful in an open cell wetsuit. Do not use it for other activities, such as surfing or SCUBA diving. Do not store the wetsuit by folding it, always hang. They can tear or become permanently creased very easily. Make sure your nails are trimmed to a short length, because they can tear the inner neoprene. Small cuts can be fixed with neoprene glue. Wetsuits are available with an open cell interior and lycra or open cell exterior. These are a little hardier. No matter how well you take care of an open cell wetsuit it just won't last as long as a closed cell wetsuit.

Smoothskin wetsuits are the least common of the three neoprene varieties. They have an open cell interior with a special coating on the exterior. They maintain all the eslasticity of open cell wetsuits. Competitive freedivers sometimes wear smoothskin suits. We recommend smoothskin suits for divers that have a long boat ride out to their dive site or are diving in significantly cold conditions. The smoothskin layer protects against wind-chill and adds extra warmth. The smoothskin layer is not especially hardy, so they are just as fragile as open cell wetsuits. The prices tend to be similar to or higher than open cell wetsuits.

Fins

Make sure your freediving fins fit properly. The foot pocket should be snug. Your heel should not easily pop out of it. If your foot pockets are frequently leaving blisters on your skin consider wearing socks. If this doesn't work sent the fins to the manufacturer and request a different size or style of foot pocket.

Fins vary in stiffness. Generally beginners start with flexible fins. They are much easier to train with. It can be hard to learn proper techniques with stiff fins. Some people recommend only using thick fins if you are above a certain weight, because it can be incredibly difficult for smaller people to move water. Some freedivers never use thick fins. It is not necessary for a long and happy freediving career.

Freediving fins are made out of three primary materials: plastic, fiberglass, and carbon fiber. Today some new companies are designing fins from bamboo and other lightweight materials, but these are the most popular and common across the world.

Plastic fins are the least expensive variety. Most entry-level freedivers begin with a pair of plastic fins. If you have ever been SCUBA diving, you used plastic fins.

Fiberglass, more durable than carbon fiber, the preferred material for many freedivers

Carbon fiber fins are the most expensive. They are incredibly lightweight and fluid. Be careful, because carbon fiber fins are very fragile. Do not store them in a bent position. When traveling keep them in a case or specialized bag.

Bi fins are the most common fins used for freediving. They are two fins that are over one meter in length. They give the freediver more power than short fins. Bi fins are versatile, because you can try different finning techniques, such as frog kicking.

Monfins are the most powerful form of fins. They look like the tail of the mermaid. Both foot pockets are connected to a single fin. With a monofin you must mermaid kick. It is easier to maneuver than it seems with a monofin.

You can use SCUBA fins for freediving. Some freedivers call these training fins. They are much easier to travel with than long freediving fins. They are almost always plastic. It is entirely possible to use closed-heel SCUBA fins as a recreational freediver. Stay away from open heel SCUBA fins for freediving, as they are not as hydrodynamic. They are helpful when exploring a fragile environment, like a coral reef or a cave full of silt. They are also useful when training in a pool where turning with long fins can be cumbersome. Long fins have more power, but proper technique gives you the most power of all.

Socks

Freediving socks reduce friction between your foot and your fins. They will also help you cover rough terrain on your way to a dive site. In an area with very hot sand or rocks, freediving socks will help you comfortably make your way to the site. If you plan on using freediving socks make sure you get fins that are a little loose.

For cold water freedivers socks are a necessity. Most freediving socks are around 2mm thick. Cold water freedivers may look for socks that are as thick as 5 or 7mm.

Weight Belt

Freedivers use weight belts to control their buoyancy underwater. Weights are typically lead and have two openings where you can thread the belt.

Always wear your weight belt around your hips, not your waist. A belt around your waist will restrict your breathing. Make sure your weight belt is snug, because your wetsuit will compress at depth. Rubber weight belts made especially for freediving are the best, because they will contract as your wetsuit compresses. The fabric weight belts made for SCUBA diving will become loose and can be cumbersome underwater. Rubber weight belts are significantly more expensive, but for those serious about freediving it is worth the investment.

Before freediving make sure you are familiar with your buddy's weight belt. In an emergency you may have to release their weight belt, so it is good to be prepared. There are a variety of fasteners available. Some of them are like a traditional belt with holes and a metal bar to clip the weight belt in place. These ones are less ideal, because you cannot always get the perfect fit. Other belts have a clip where you can thread the belt and pull to your desired fit. All belts are designed with a quick-release system, so they are easy to ditch in an emergency.

If there is slack on your belt make sure you tuck it in a way that is still quick-release. Simply tucking the excess into the belt may be difficult to undo in an emergency. Instead fold the excess and tuck the fold into the belt. There should be a loop coming through the top with the end coming out at the bottom. Pulling on the end should undo your loop and release the weight belt.

Nose Clip

To prevent water from entering the nose many
freedivers use nose clips. Nose clips work well under
numerous situations. Some divers prefer to do static
breath holds without a mask and only a nose clip.
While reaching depths a nose clip is useful, because
you won't need to pinch your nose to equalize.
Sometimes divers wear specialized fluid-filled goggles
with their nose clip, so they can still see and they
won't need to equalize the air space in front of the
eyes. Competitive freedivers dive with a nose clip.
This saves oxygen by not having to pinch their nose
and they eliminate the need to equalize the air space
of the mask.

Buoy

While training in the ocean most freedivers use a
buoy. It is good to recover from deep dives on a
flotation device. This gives you extra support.
Freediving buoys are circular and house a line, bottom
weight, carabiner, and a lanyard. The length of the
line will be determined by the experience and training
level of the freedivers. The bottom weight is tied to the
line (usually with a knot called a bowline). Bottom
weights usually weigh between 8 to 10 kilos. The line
is fastened to the buoy with a strong carabiner. The
line will have marking on it to signal various lengths.
The bottom of the line will have marks to tell the diver
that they are near the bottom. See, there's no reason
to look down at depth. If you are preparing your own
freediving line use ink rather than tape to create these
marks. Tape may snag a lanyard and cause
unnecessary stress underwater. Always keep your chin
tucked. Make sure the carabiner that you tie the line

to can hold your body weight. Also make sure it will not corrode in salt water.

The lanyard is a piece of equipment that attaches a freediver to their buoy. A lanyard will give you peace of mind while diving. You can close your eyes, relax, and rest assured that you are descending and ascending with the line. A carabiner will clip them into the line and they diver will attach a Velcro strap onto their wrist, ankle, or weight belt. The line on a freediving lanyard is made of a special material that is difficult to tangle. It is okay to do your warmup dives without a lanyard, but once you start going deep be sure to wear a lanyard. Only one diver should wear the lanyard. If both the diver and the safety diver wear lanyards it can result in entanglement and confusion.

Choose a buoy that is a strong color of orange, red, or yellow. This will help you stand out to boat traffic. It is also a good idea to attach a dive flag to your buoy. Check your local regulations to see what flag signals boats that there are divers below. Usually it is a red rectangle with a white diagonal line.

Buoys are also helpful to store cameras, water bottles, and debris you find in the ocean.

Knife

Recreational freedivers should carry a knife. This is a life-saving piece of equipment in case of entanglement. When freediving in an area notorious for fishing it is an especially good idea to carry a knife.

Even if you don't become entangled you will be able to free corals, sea grass, and other marine life that are tangled in fishing line. Some knives are equipped with a special line-cutting hook. SCUBA shops will sell knives with sheaths that can be strapped onto your arm or leg. Choose the most hydrodynamic and comfortable model.

Gloves

There are many reasons a freediver would choose to wear gloves. Gloves can be helpful when pulling up the line onto the buoy. Cold water divers will require gloves to keep them warm. Gloves are available in various thicknesses, so choose the model that will keep you warm. Spearfishers and lobster divers also use gloves to protect themselves against spines. Some gloves have thick patches of strong material and other gloves are sleek and hydrodynamic. Choose something that matches what you're doing underwater.

Watch

A good freediving watch includes a depth gauge, time, and logbook. Additional features include a thermometer and electronic compass. Some watches allow you to set an alarm at a certain depth. This can be helpful to remind you to freefall or change equalization techniques.

For SCUBA divers choose a dive computer that is compatible with both freediving and SCUBA diving.

Sunscreen

The most common injury from freediving is sunburn. Luckily, this is easy to prevent. Apply sunscreen before diving. Avoid the face, because it may run into your eyes and sting when it gets wet. Sunscreen may also damage your mask.

Be careful when applying sunscreen on your wrists, because some dive watch materials are sensitive to the chemicals in sunscreen. Excessive exposure to sunscreen may damage the watch.

Another way to prevent sunburn is to cover your skin. Use a full body rashguard, gloves, hood, and socks.

Always buy sunscreen that is reef safe. Check the label for oxybenzone, octocrylene, 4MBC, butylparaben, and octinoxate. If it has any of these chemicals put it back on the shelf and choose a different brand. Choose sunscreen that is based on zinc oxide or titanium dioxide. It is a good idea to use reef safe sunscreen even when you are far away from the ocean, because the water cycle will carry all chemicals into the ocean eventually.

Chapter 9: Proper Weighting

Finding your balance underwater

The Freediving Weight Check

It is a good idea to be neutrally buoyant with full lungs at 1/3 of your target depth (or deeper). This will give you the ability to safely control your ascent and descent. When you are neutrally buoyant you will feel weightless underwater. This is a good depth to explore and enjoy recreational freediving.

Perform a weight check at this depth during your warm up dives. To perform a weight check descend with full lungs, stop at the target depth, do not hold onto the line, and observe. Your body should hover neutrally buoyant. You are neutrally buoyant when you are neither sinking nor floating. SCUBA divers will have a good sense of this. Usually, with full lungs and without a wetsuit, most people are neutrally buoyant at 10 meters in salt water.

For safety reasons make sure you are positively buoyant at the surface. This will help you relax before a dive. You should be able to comfortably inhale and exhale without sinking.

Remember that in fresh water you will require less weight than in salt water. This is because freshwater is less dense than water with salt in it. The amount of weights you use will also vary depending on wetsuit thickness and body composition.

Using your Buoyancy

As pressure increases, your buoyancy decreases. At depth your lungs and wetsuit will compress. This will make you negatively buoyant. Use this to your advantage by free falling. We will go into more details about free falling in the upcoming chapters.

As pressure decreases, your buoyancy increases. As you ascend your lungs will re-inflate with air and your wetsuit will decompress. You will begin to float up to the surface. Use this to your advantage by limiting your movements (which burn O2).

We will go into more detail about these concepts in future chapters.

The Dangers of Overweighting

It may be tempting to use a lot of weights while freediving, but be careful. It can be very dangerous to don too much weight underwater. You may use too much energy on ascent. Your buddy will have a more difficult time rescuing you in an emergency if you're overweighted. Overweighting can also cause you to reach depths you are not comfortable descending to yet.

Chapter 10: Duck Dive

Starting your Descent

What is a Duck Dive?

Freedivers initiate descent by performing something called a duck dive. A successful duck dive will send you 2-5 meters deep. Duck dives are primarily used for recreational freediving and constant weight freediving. They are not used for free immersion. You will learn more about freediving disciplines in later chapters.

Technique

To begin a freedive use the duck dive. A well-performed duck dive allows you to glide effortlessly into the deep. It utilizes the weight of your body and position of your arms to push you deeper into the ocean. Remember that would will be positively buoyant at the surface. Without a proper duck dive it takes a lot of effort to break through the first pressure gradients.

1. Position arms over your head
2. Kick for momentum (on surface)
3. Pre-equalize
4. Bend at the hip
5. Raise feet over torso
6. Allow yourself to sink
7. Take one strong arm stroke

8. Keep arms by your side
9. Allow yourself to sink
10. Start finning.

If you are freediving with a buoy start your momentum kicks a little to the side and behind the float. Keep the buoy on the side of your body with the lanyard. This way you can descend right in front of the line after your momentum kicks.

Recreational Freediving

Duck dives are incredible useful when you are just diving for fun. It will help you peek beneath shallow rocks or begin a descent down a coral wall. The more you recreationally freedive, the easier your duck dive will become, and the more comfortable you will be when diving on a line.

Chapter 11: Swimming Techniques

Moving through the Underwater World

Technique

While freediving always look straight ahead. For many people this may feel unnatural. It may feel like your chin is tucked in, when in fact you are looking up. Do not focus on where you are going. Focus on the water directly in front of you. Looking up makes you significantly less hydrodynamic. It bends your back like a banana. Instead of going straight your path will begin to veer. It is also much easier to relax when you're looking straight ahead. At depth it is dangerous to look up. By tucking your chin in you are protecting your trachea from being squeezed.

At depths greater than 25 meters you will want to hunch your shoulders over. This will protect your lungs from being squeezed.

You have two choices for where to keep your hands while freediving. First, you can keep them by your side. This is the most common. The closer you keep your hands to your thighs, the most hydrodynamic you will be. Second, you can keep them above your head. Imagine your body is an arrow piercing through the water. This style is commonly used for mermaid kicking. Keeping your arms above your head is also good for recreational freediving to ensure that you don't swim into anything.

In many cases a snorkel is handy while freediving. It can help you observe corals while swimming out to the dive site or relax in choppy conditions. It does help on the surface, but you should never have your snorkel in your mouth underwater. Either spit it out and swim with it attached to your mask or take it off entirely. You will be more hydrodynamic without a snorkel.

If your snorkel is in your mouth underwater it can lead to some dangerous scenarios. When you return to the surface your first instinct will be to purge the snorkel with one big exhale. This is dangerous, because your body should be recovering from the breath hold with a lot of air in the lungs to promote gas exchange. By exhaling a lot of air very quickly your oxygen levels will drop. This may lead to a blackout on the surface if the dive was strenuous. Also, if you black out the snorkel the snorkel may act like a straw. The influx of water you're your mouth can undo your body's natural reflex against inhaling water (the laryngospasm).

Mermaid

Mermaid kicking is exactly as it sounds- kicking as if you have a mermaid tail. Your torso should stay still while your hips move back and forth. Mermaid kicking is all about the rhythm of your kicks. Make each movement smooth and powerful. Usually divers keep their hand above their head. It uses a lot of core strength. Many people feel that mermaid kicking is the most natural way to move through the water.

The most challenging part of mermaid kicking is finding equilibrium. You should kick as much forward as you do backwards. Most people are naturally inclined to kick more in one direction. Break this habit by training in a pool. Do not bend your knees while finning, but rather let the motion come from your hips. It can be helpful for a friend to record a video of your dive, so you can see exactly what your form looks like underwater. Remember to look straight ahead and keep your chin tucked in.

For a more powerful mermaid kick, use a monofin. Monofins significantly increase the surface area of the water you are pushing.

Bi-Finning

Bi-finning is the most common finning technique amongst freedivers. Kick from your hips and try to keep your legs as straight as possible. If you're bending your knees the fin blades will slice through the water instead of push it. Finning with bent knees is very ineffective. Point your toes to get as much power as possible from your fins.

For this kick you should also find equilibrium. Your kicks should be about the length of your average step, forwards and backwards.

Kick at a slow, smooth rhythm. Allow yourself to glide between the kicks.

No Fins

Some people think of no fins as the most natural form of freediving. No fin freedivers only use a wetsuit, weight belt, mask or nose clip. They use their upper and lower body strength to push themselves through the water.

To do a no fins arm stroke start with your hands by your side. Bring them up in front of your body with your palms facing in and hands touching. This movement should be smooth. You should keep your hands close to your body to be more hydrodynamic. Extend your arms as high up as you can, then twist your palms outwards. Now push the water. Slightly bend your elbows. If you don't bend your elbows your figure will be very wide in the water and less hydrodynamic. Once your arms reach just below your shoulders change your stroke. Bring your hands in then push down powerfully. The entire movement should look like the outline of an arrowhead. It starts pointy, then becomes wider, moves in, then pushes down. You can practice this stroke on dry land first.

After each arm strokes, when your arms return to your sides, perform one or two kicks. These kicks should be kind of like a frog. First flex your feet. Then push the water outwards. Completely extend your knees. Bring your feet back together. Point your toes between kicks to become more hydrodynamic.

For no fins freediving you should have flexibility in your chest, shoulders, and hips.

Free Fall

Free falling is the favorite part of any dive for most freedivers. Once you reach a depth where you are negatively buoyant you can start to free fall. Make your last kick or pull extra powerful to initiate the descent. Keep your eyes looking straight ahead and tuck your chin in slightly. Point your toes to be more hydrodynamic. Place your arms by your side, touching your thighs. Focus on becoming hydrodynamic. Clear your mind to use less oxygen. The only movement you need to make while free falling is equalizing. It may seem like you aren't moving, but if you're negatively buoyant you surely are. Trust the free fall. Implement the same form on your ascent when you are positively buoyant.

You can descend very far with exerting very little energy. Free falling really helps the diver conserve oxygen on descent.

Chapter 12: The Turn

Ending your Descent and Beginning your Ascent

When to Turn?

Most freediving buoys have a bottom plate, tennis ball, or some other signaling device to tell you when you have reached your target depth. Relax on your descent, dive within your limits, and you will easily find yourself at the bottom of the line. Then it is time to go back up.

If you are having troubles equalizing or feel yourself pushing your limits then it is time to turn. You can turn on any point on the rope when you begin to feel uncomfortable.

Turning with Proper Form

A good turn should use minimum effort. When you are nearing the turning point extend one arm (if you are wearing a lanyard extend the arm with the lanyard on it). Most freediving lines will have marks to signal when you're approaching the end of the line. When you reach the point at which you wish to turn simply grad the line. This will stop your descent. It is best to grab with your thumb pointing towards the surface, so you don't have to readjust as you turn. Now begin a forward tumble. Arch your back forward and let the rest of your body follow. When you are ready to start your ascent give the line a nice pull.

Even if you have done a constant weight descent, it is good practice to give the line one strong pull when you are turning. We will go into more detail about different freediving disciplines in the last chapter. The pull will boost you up and make your ascent easier and you have to grab the line anyway to turn. Remember, you will usually be negatively buoyant when you're turning.

Always use the same form on your turns, no matter how shallow. Make good technique a habit to avoid injury.

Safety

It is absolutely essential that you arch your back inwards, keep your shoulders hunched, and tuck your chin in. Always do a forward tuck turn. Otherwise you are putting yourself at risk for a lung or throat squeeze. Correct form will protect your body.

Chapter 13: Ascent

Returning to the Surface

Use your Buoyancy

As discussed before you will become more positively buoyant as you head back up towards the surface. The top 1/3 of your dive should be absolutely effortless. This is because you should be positively buoyant.

Equalizing

There is no reason to equalize on ascent. While descending our airspaces shrink, but on ascent our air spaces expand. The excess air will escape naturally.

You will notice bubbles escaping your mask as the pressure decreases. To conserve air inhale this air before it escapes.

Recovering

Before exhaling on the surface grab onto something for support. In a pool use the edge and in the ocean use a buoy. Exhale. Start recovery breathing and signal to your buddy that you are okay. Do not speak while recovery breathing. Instead use a hand signal. The universal sign for "I am okay" is to touch your pointer finger to your thumb.

Chapter 14: Advancing your Dives

Building a Tolerance to Apnea

CO2 Tables

CO2 tables will help you condition your body to function with high levels of CO2. They work by gradually decreasing the amount of preparation time between breath holds. Remember to do recovery breaths after each breath hold. Each breath hold is 50% of your static personal best. You may notice that the first breath hold is the most difficult, because your mammalian dive reflex is yet to kick in. To increase your body's ability to withstand apnea complete one CO2 table six days a week. You will notice dramatic improvement to your static breath hold times, dynamic distances, and overall comfort underwater.

It is completely safe to practice CO2 tables on your own if you are dry. Remember that dry breath holds will always be more difficult than when submerged. Your mammalian dive reflex is weaker when you are dry. When you are training in a pool or the ocean make sure you have a buddy to watch you. It is very unlikely to black out during a CO2 table, because your Oxygen levels are not dropping that much. Even so, it is wise to always have supervision when holding your breath underwater.

Do not attempt a personal best for static apnea after completing a carbon dioxide table. Your carbon dioxide levels will be very high, so it better to do this before.

Here is a sample CO2 table:

PREP	HOLD
2:00	50% of PB
1:45	50% of PB
1:30	50% of PB
1:15	50% of PB
1:00	50% of PB
:45	50% of PB
:30	50% of PB
:15	50% of PB

O2 Tables

O2 levels decrease your oxygen levels, so you can build a stronger tolerance to low oxygen. The improvement you will notice from O2 tables is much less dramatic than CO2 tables. Usually these are performed by competitive freedivers. It is better to focus on CO2 tables for most freedivers.

The risk of blacking out is much higher when performing O2 tables, because your O2 levels become really low. Always use the buddy system when you are in water. Don't forget your recovery breaths. They are especially important when you are low on oxygen.

During an O2 table do not do any breath holds that exceed 80% of your personal best. Adjust the times if necessary. Here is a sample O2 table:

PREP	HOLD
2:00	1:00
2:00	1:15
2:00	1:30
2:00	1:45
2:00	2:00
2:00	2:15
2:00	2:30
2:00	2:45

Depth Increases

As you plan on going deeper and deeper, take things gradually. You must give your body time to adjust

Preparing for Freediving

There are a number of stretching and breathing techniques that can make our modies more flexible and better-adapted to reach depths.

Stretching the intercoastal muscles will increase your lung volume. Stand with your feet shoulder-width apart, raise one arm over your head and reach as far as you can. To improve your lung capacity take one full breath, then hold this pose. Be careful and do not push yourself and your breath holds too far when stretching. Be aware of your body and monitor yourself for dizziness. After each breath hold you should be performing recovery breaths.

Kapalabhati is a helpful technique to release congestion and prepare the sinuses for equalization. Cover one nostril, inhale passively, and exhale 'explosively'. Repeat 10-15 times for each nostril. Breaths should come from your belly. This technique is also called 'Skull-Shining'.

Jaw stretches are also good for equalization. The best jaw stretch is called the 'Camel Stretch'. This is because it is similar to how a camel chews its food. Move your jaw first to the right as far as you can, then down as far as you can, then to the left as far as you can. Repeat in the other direction. You should feel some movement, and maybe equalization, in your ears.

Brahmari breathing will also help relieve congestion. Breathe out of your nose on your exhales and make a sound that sounds like bees. The vibrations will help loosen the mucus in your sinuses. This is also very good for relaxation, so it is good to do before diving.

Freedivers should work to keep their shoulders and chest open. Practice by placing your arms over your head, like an arrow, and leaning onto a doorway. You should feel the stretch in your shoulders. This is especially helpful for those who wish to begin mermaid kicking.

Uddiyana Banda

Uddiyana Banda is the best stretch for freedivers. It comes from hatha yoga. At a certain depth our lungs shrink so much that the volume is less than that after we exhale fully. This is called the residual volume. Uddiyana Banda makes the diaphragm more flexible and allows it to contract more at depth. This will make your dives deeper and more comfortable. When the diaphragm is able to move up further you will no longer feel a strong pressure on your chest.

To perform Uddiyana Banda follow these steps:

1. Start with your feet shoulder width apart. You can also perform the exercise in a sitting down criss-cross position if that is more comfortable for you.
2. Relax your body and exhale fully.
3. Bend forward to empty the lungs completely. Your upper body weight should be on your hands. Support yourself on your knees or upper thighs.

4. Keep your chin tucked in. This is important to prevent throat injury.
5. With your epiglottis closed make your chest full. Do not inhale. Your diaphragm should be rising as you do this.
6. Hold this position for as long as you're comfortable. Do not wait until you start to get contractions.
7. After Uddiyana Banda perform recovery breaths, just like you should after every breath hold.

Perform Uddiyana Banda 5-6 times a week at 5-10 times a session. It is good to do right before freediving to help your body relax as well.

Nauli kriya is a powerful stretch for those who have mastered Uddiyana Banda. It massages the stomach, liver, spleen, intestines, and other lower body organs. When performing Uddiyanna Banda try to identify feeling in your two abdominal muscle columns. This will take patience and practice. Once you can identify the muscles, consciously push one outwards. Retract and push the other outwards. Others will see a visible movement in your abdomen. No breathing occurs during the process. This is a challenging stretch with great benefits. Ask a yoga instructor for advice if you are keen to learn.

Chapter 15: Freediving Disciplines

Different Kinds of Freediving to Expand your Training and Understand Competitions

Static Apnea (STA)

Static apnea involves holding your breath face down in water. You can do static apnea in a pool or in confined water, like a calm bay or lake. Static apnea is good to practice as it will help you with all disciplines of freediving. It makes you more comfortable with contractions and the urge to breathe. It will also help you better understand your limits and measure your improvement as a freediver. It can help build mindfulness and meditation skills.

Remember to hold on to the pool edge and perform recovery breaths after every breath hold.

Static apnea is the most accessible form of freediving. Even those in a big city far from any body of water can practice in a pool. Check in your area for freediving groups, because often in many areas people meet to train in gyms or other venues.

Dynamic Apnea (DYN) (DNF)

Dynamic apnea is when the diver covers horizontal distances on one breath. Traditionally this is completed in a pool and the diver has to turn on either end.

There are two disciplines in dynamic apnea. DYN is when the diver uses either bi-fins or monofins. Usually competitors will use monofins, because they are more efficient. DNF is when the diver uses no fins. This involves a strong arm stroke and duck kicking. It is very demanding.

Dynamic apnea requires near perfect buoyancy. If you are too heavy you will be struggling to stay off the bottom of the pool. If you are too light you will be using extra energy to stay away from the surface. With perfect buoyancy you will glide through the water. Sometimes dynamic apnea divers use neck weights. A neck weight counter balances the buoyancy of the lungs, so they can be streamlined in shallow water.

No matter what kind of freediving you do, it is good to practice dynamic apnea. It is easy to correct your form, finning techniques, and posture while training in a pool. It is also a good way to improve your CO_2 tolerance. Just remember, if you push yourself or hyperventilate you are just as likely to black out in a pool as in the ocean.

Free Immersion (FIM)

Free immersion is when a freediver descends and ascends by pulling themselves on a line. Most divers find this discipline to be relaxing. Freedivers usually start their sessions by warming up with free immersion dives. This is a good way to keep lactic acid from building up in your legs. In a freediving course this is probably the first diving method that will be introduced to you. It is easy to go slowly and take your time equalizing.

You can train for free immersion with fins, as it is easier to alternate turns with your buddy. In competitions free immersion divers are not allowed to wear fins.

Constant Weight (CWT) (CNF)

Constant weight involves the diver swimming down and up with the same amount of weight.

CWT includes freedivers wearing bi-fins and monofins. Monofins are more powerful, so the top records are held by monofin divers. CNF is constant weight diving with no fins. This discipline gets more media attention than any other freediving discipline.

In competitions freedivers are only allowed to grab the rope as they are turning at the bottom.

Variable Weight (VWT)

Variable weight freediving is when the freediver uses a weight to aid their descent. Sometimes this is in the form of a traditional weight and other times it is sled hat the diver holds onto. The freediver is required to ascent without weights. Usually variable weight divers in competitions do not wear weight belts, so the buoyancy of their wetsuit and full lungs aids their ascent efforts. They may become positively buoyant very deep. The diver may pull on the rope, swim, or both during their ascent.

Sometimes freedivers start their training session with a variable weight dive. They will set up the buoy and go down with the bottom weight. It is important to have good, rapid equalization technique before attempting a variable weight dive. Never attempt if you are congested.

Variable weight diving is much riskier than other freediving disciplines. It is not recognized in competitions by some freediving governing bodies, because of the associated risks.

No Limits (NLT)

No limits is when the freediver descends on a weighted sled and ascends using a lifting device. Usually this is a balloon or lift bag that the diver fills once they reach their target depth. This is the most potentially dangerous of all freediving disciplines. Competitions are no longer held for no limits diving due to the risk factors.

No limits is still practiced for fun and training by some divers. It should definitely never be attempted if you are suffering from even minor congestion.

Recreational Freediving

This is the most fun form of freediving. It is when you explore the ocean, lakes, rivers, caverns, and other underwater realms on one breath. Always use the buddy system. Use a one-up-one-down policy when recreationally freediving. This means while you are freediving your buddy should be on the surface watching you, and vice versa. Keep your depth to 50% of your personal best. Make sure you give yourself adequate time to rest between dives and perform recovery breaths after each breath hold. Typically you won't use a buoy while recreationally freediving. Remember to respect all underwater life, for that is their home and you are only a visitor.

About the Expert

Julie Shoults is passionate about freediving. This passion has taken her all over the world to freedive in remarkable places. She is a PADI SCUBA and Freediving Instructor. Julie is from Florida in the United States, but now she is a world traveler. Julie started her freediving journey in the Middle East where she was working as a SCUBA Instructor. It is with a lot of patience and Vitamin Sea that she gradually improves her freediving practice. She has been freediving in the beautiful lakes of East Africa, with whale sharks, turtles, manta rays, and on countless coral reefs. At the time of publication she is living in Bali, Indonesia, where she can reach depths right from the shore! Her goal is to study science and continue traveling.

Follow her adventure on Instagram: @JulieShoults

HowExpert publishes quick 'how to' guides on all topics from A to Z by everyday experts. Visit HowExpert.com to learn more.

Recommended Resources

- HowExpert.com – Quick 'How To' Guides on All Topics from A to Z by Everyday Experts.
- HowExpert.com/free – Free HowExpert Email Newsletter.
- HowExpert.com/books – HowExpert Books
- HowExpert.com/courses – HowExpert Courses
- HowExpert.com/membership – HowExpert Membership Site
- HowExpert.com/writers – Write About Your #1 Passion/Knowledge/Expertise & Become a HowExpert Author.
- HowExpert.com/resources – Additional HowExpert Recommended Resources
- YouTube.com/HowExpert – Subscribe to HowExpert YouTube.
- Instagram.com/HowExpert – Follow HowExpert on Instagram.
- Facebook.com/HowExpert – Follow HowExpert on Facebook.

CPSIA information can be obtained
at www.ICGtesting.com
Printed in the USA
FSHW021510020321
79106FS